Do You Like

Bitch?

Beautiful Swear Word To Color

For Stress Releasing

Chase C. Demon

Happy Coloring!

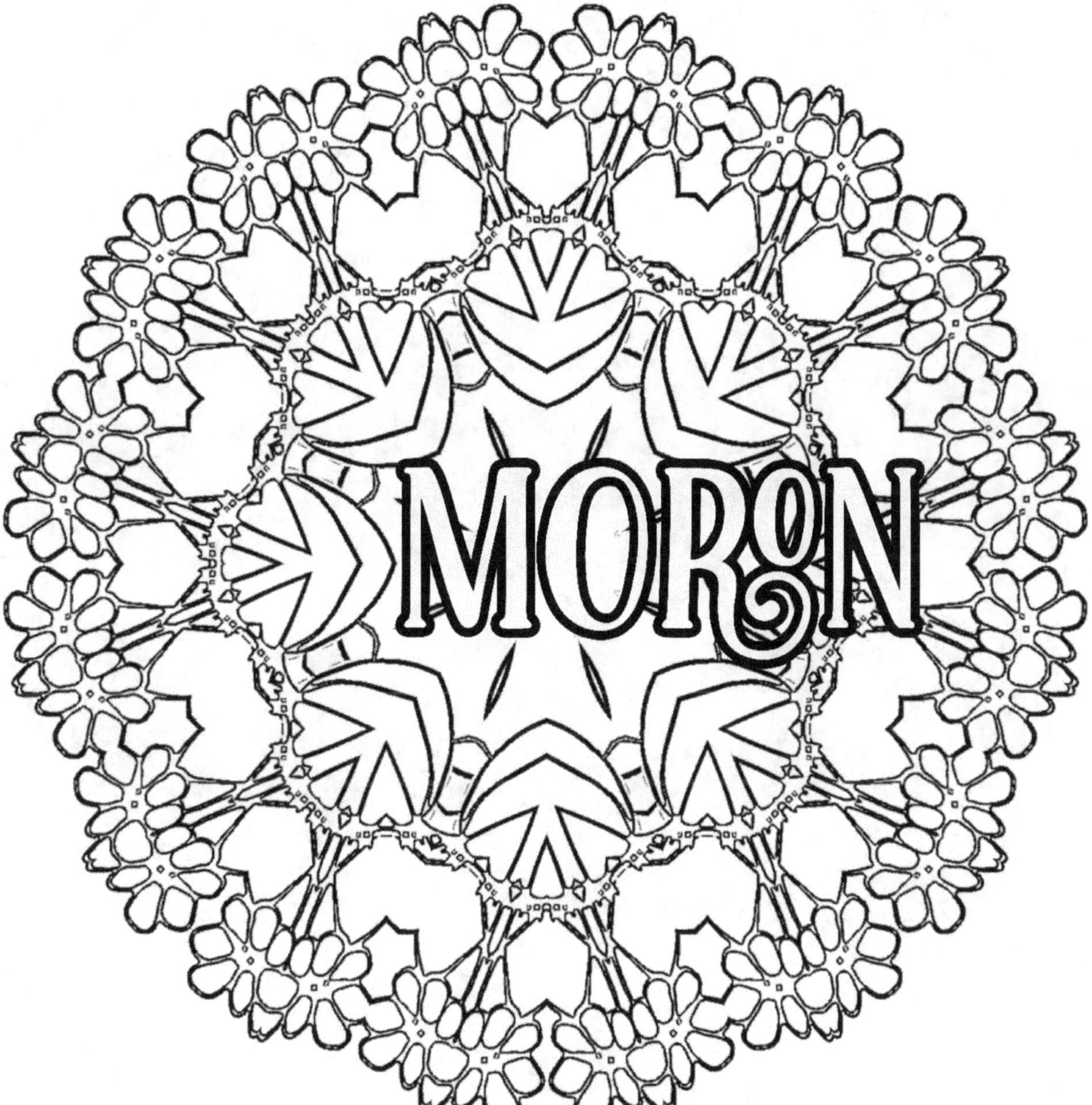
MORON

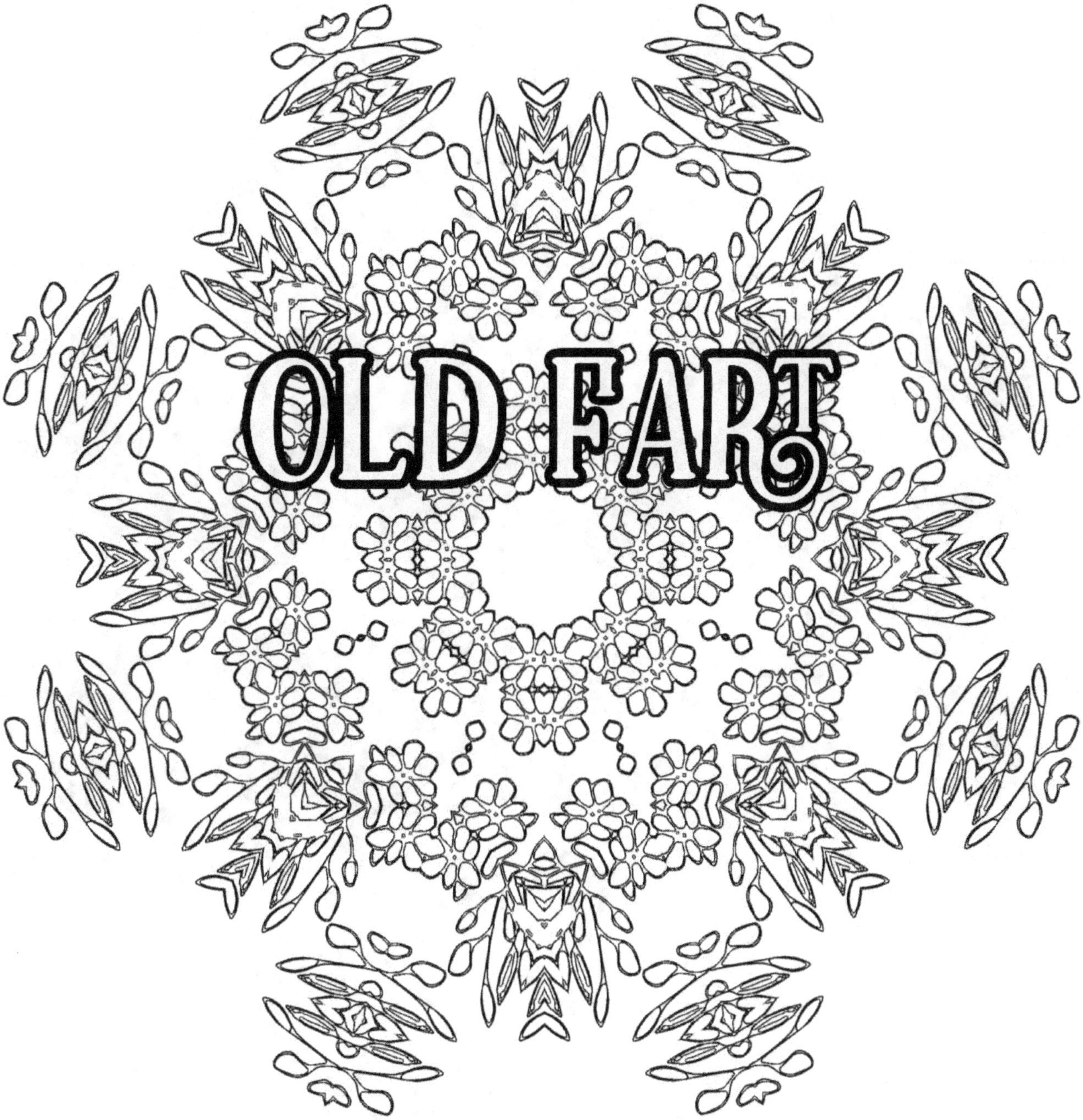
OLD FART

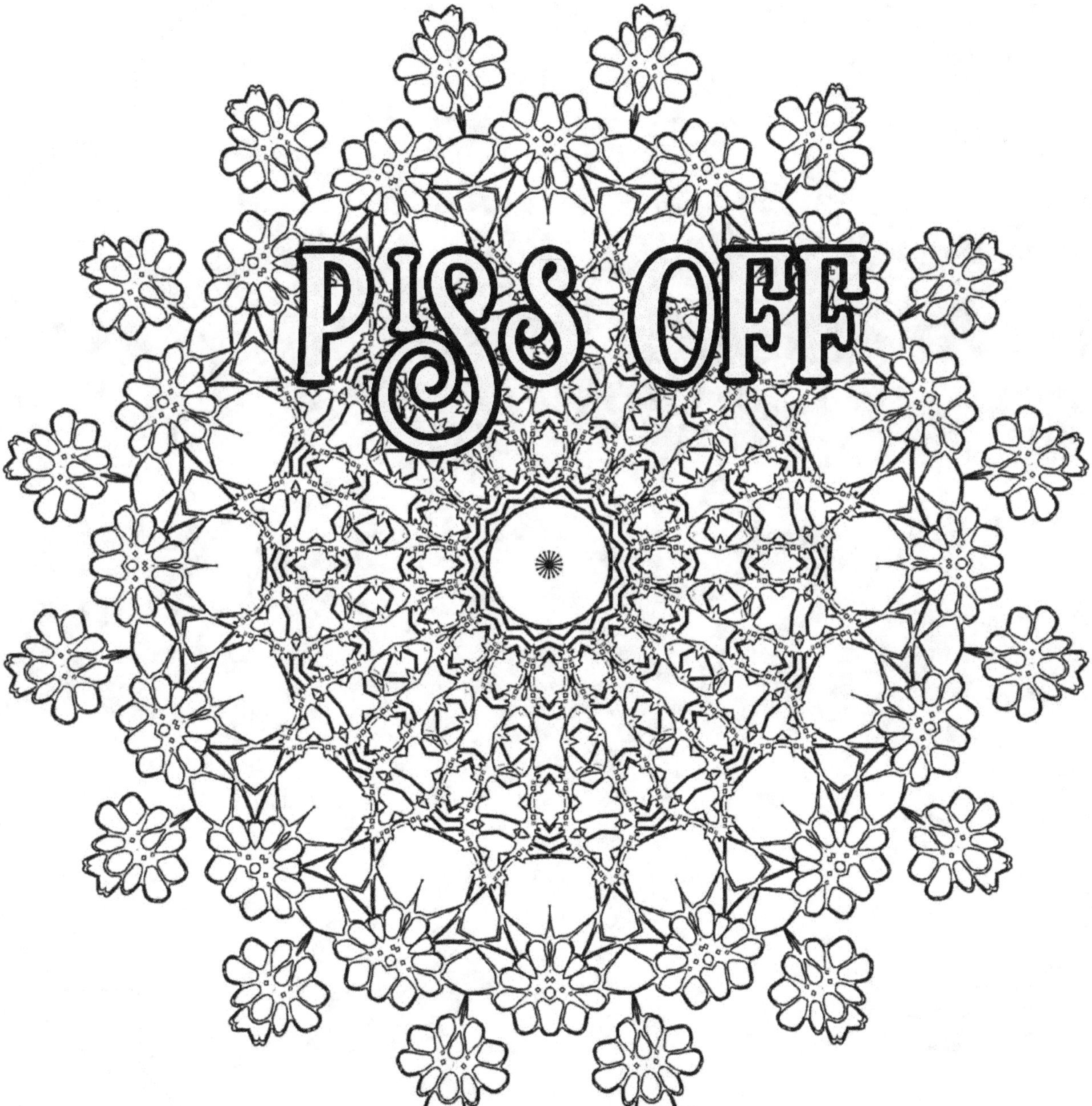
PISS OFF

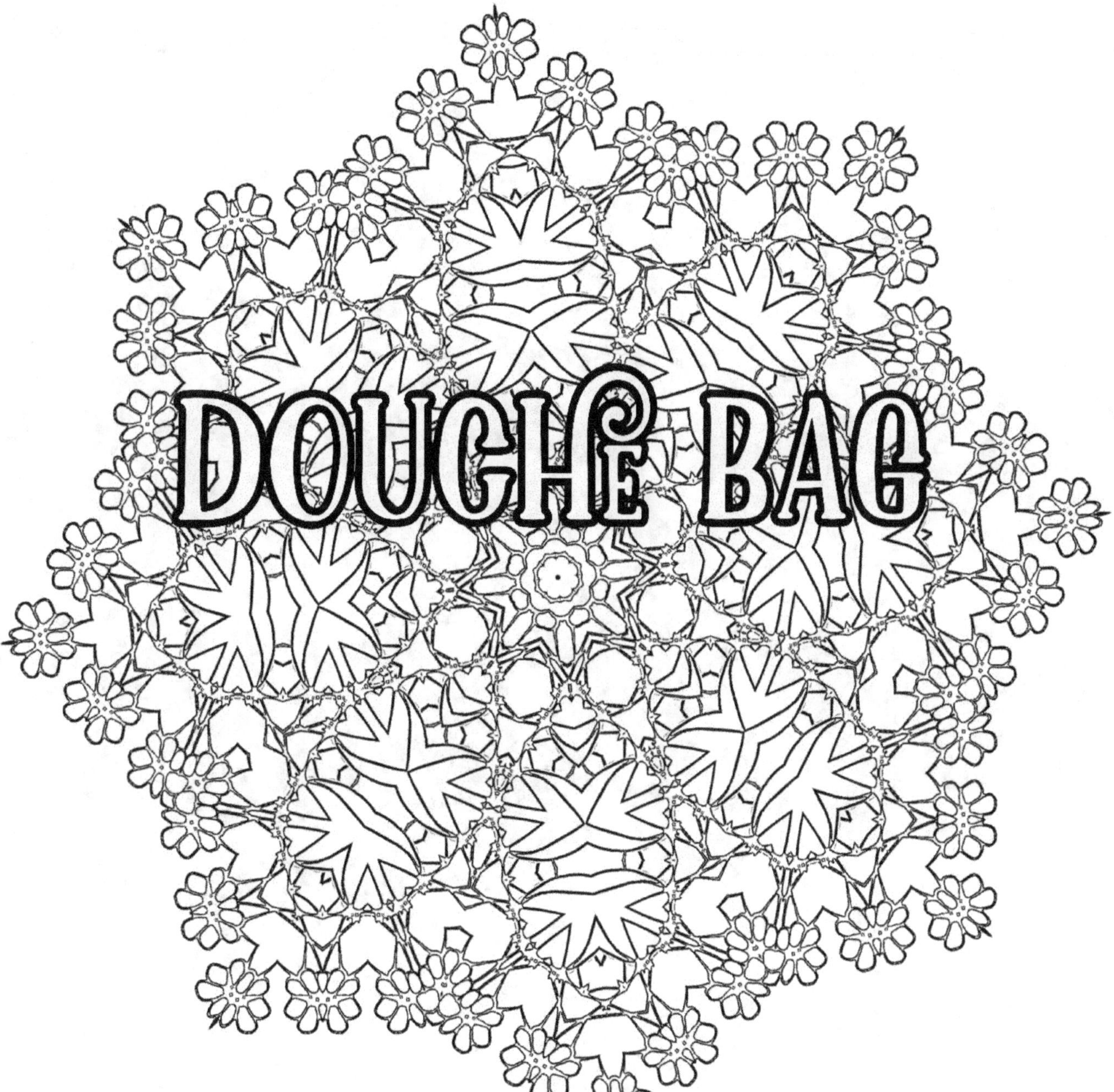
DOUCHE BAG

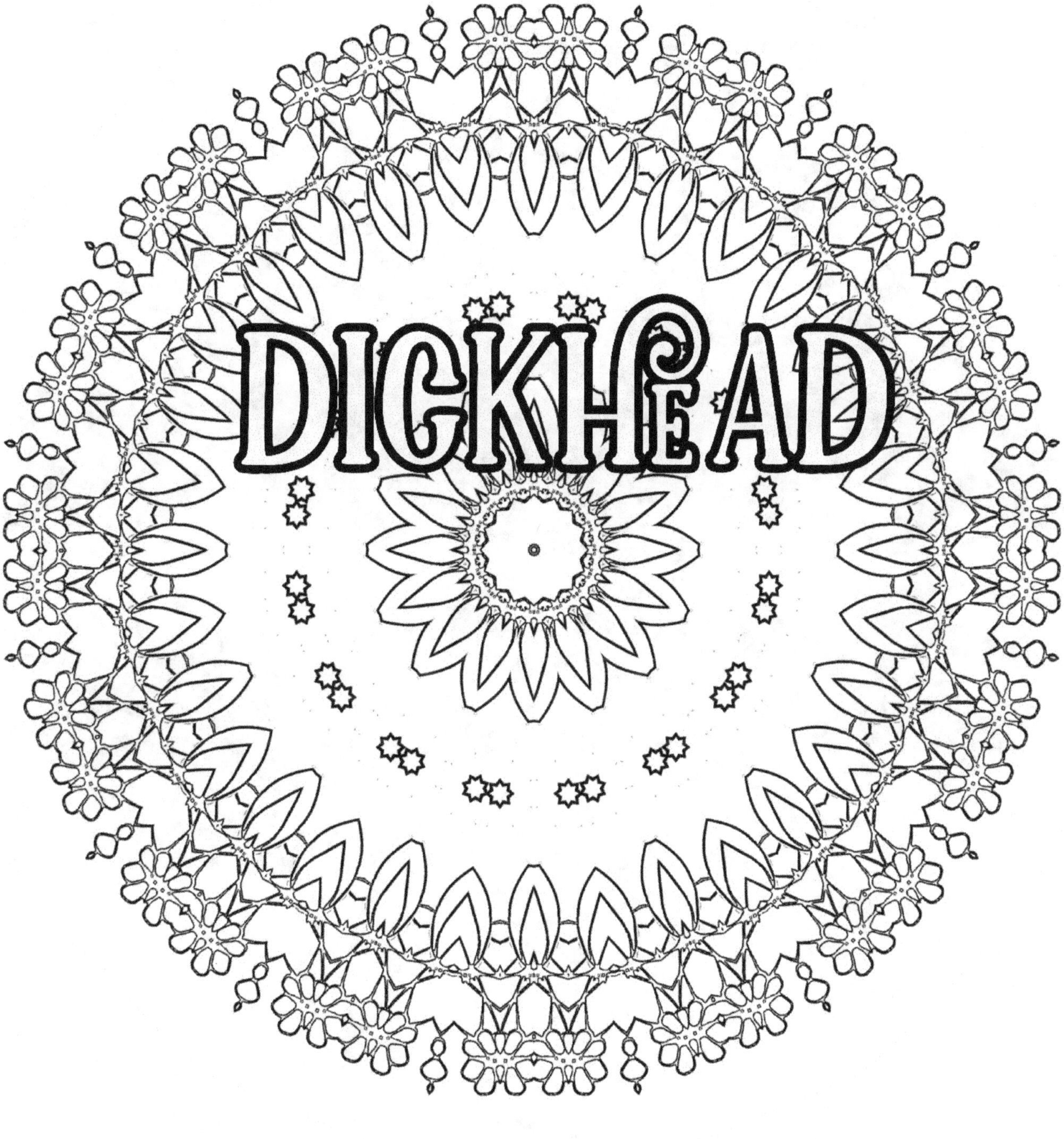
DICKHEAD

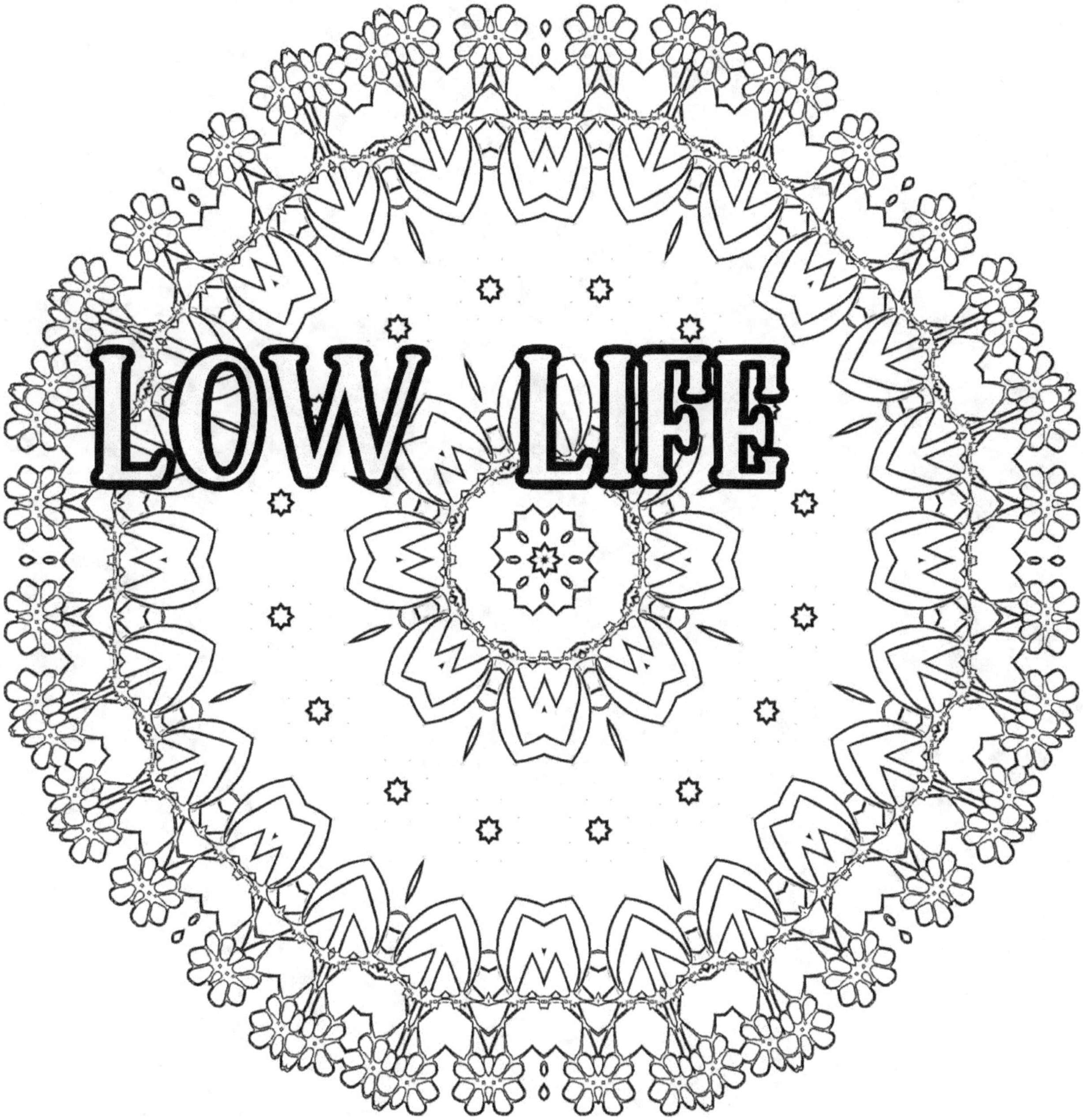
LOW LIFE

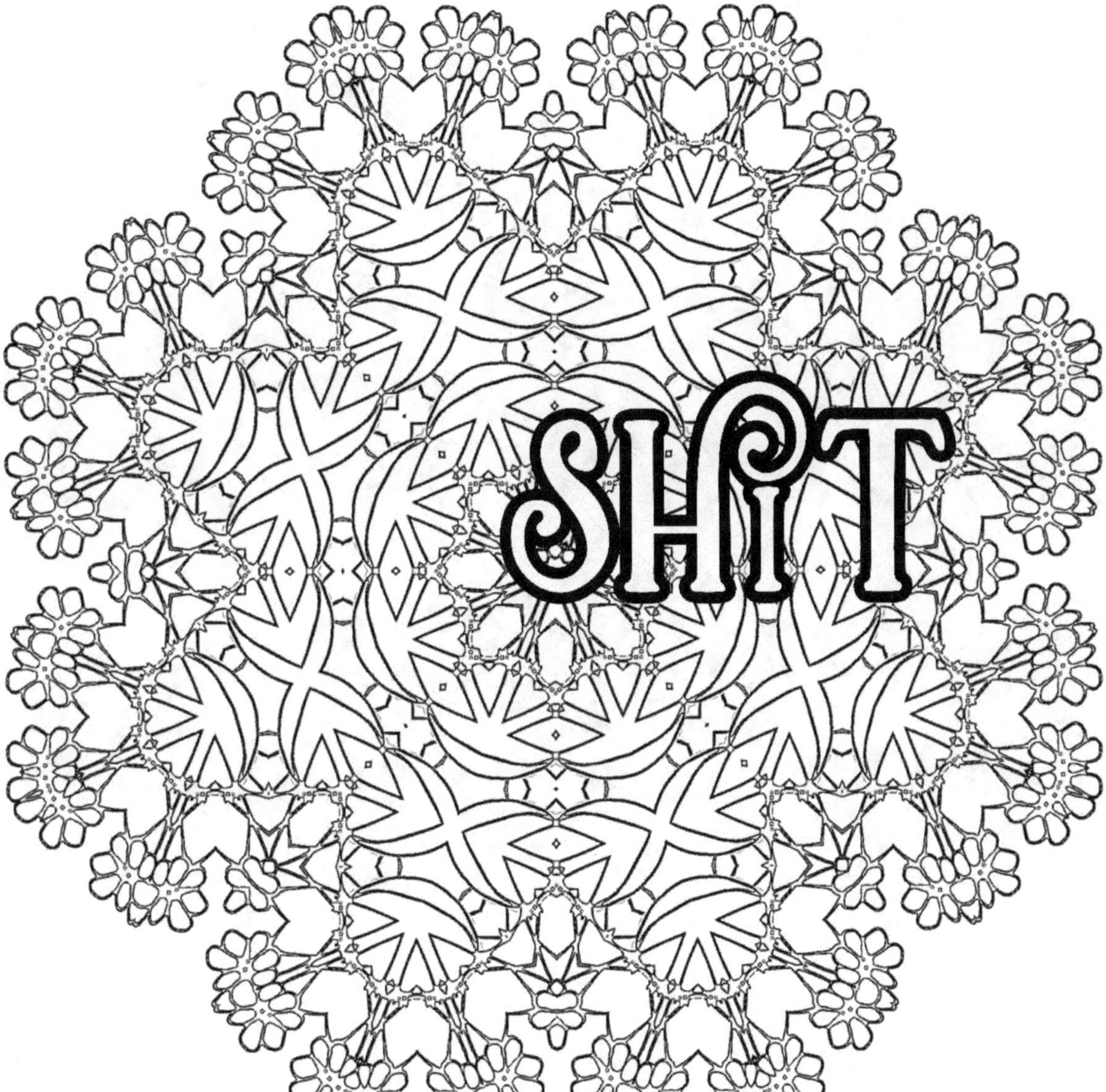
SHIT

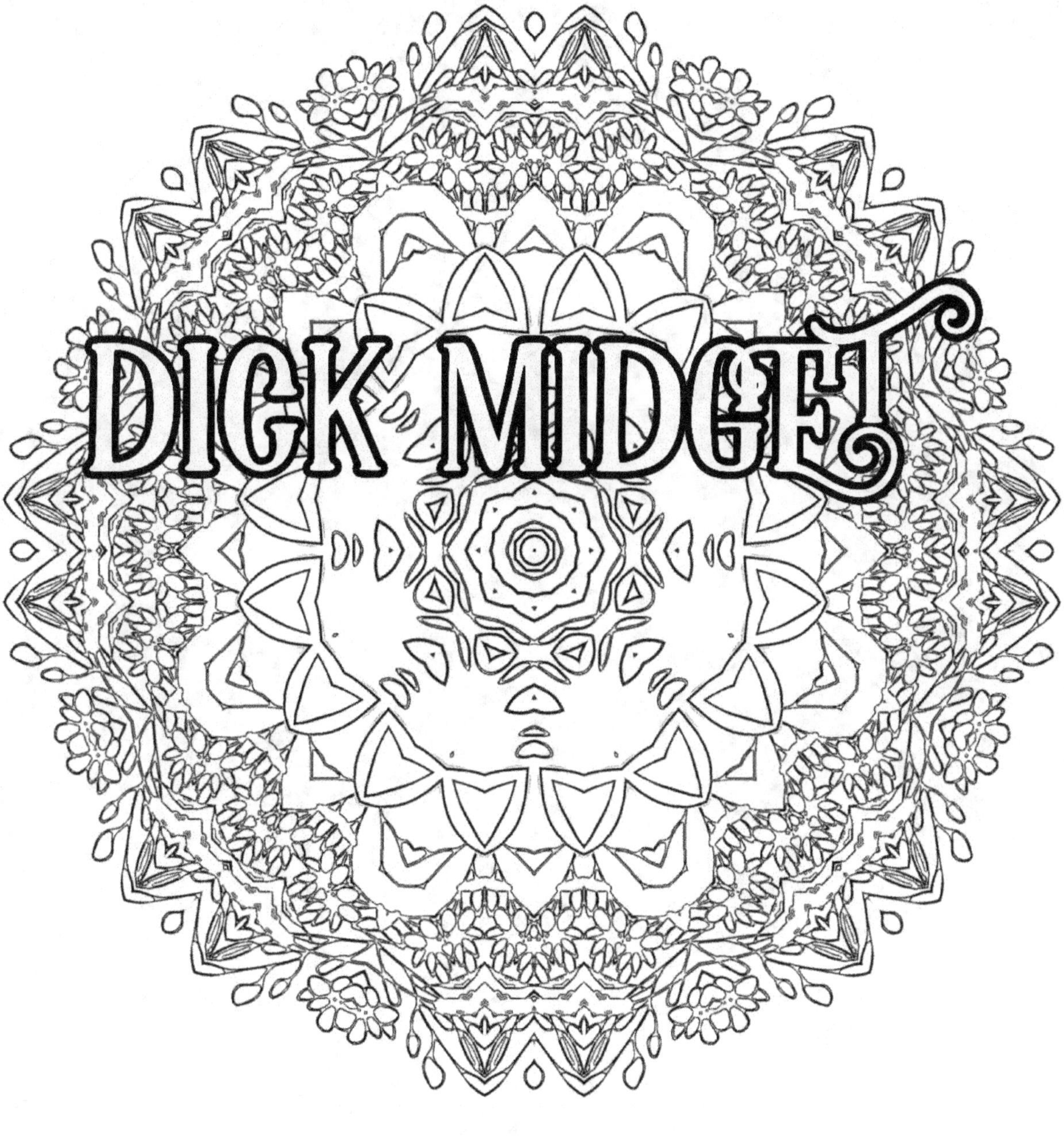
DICK MIDGET

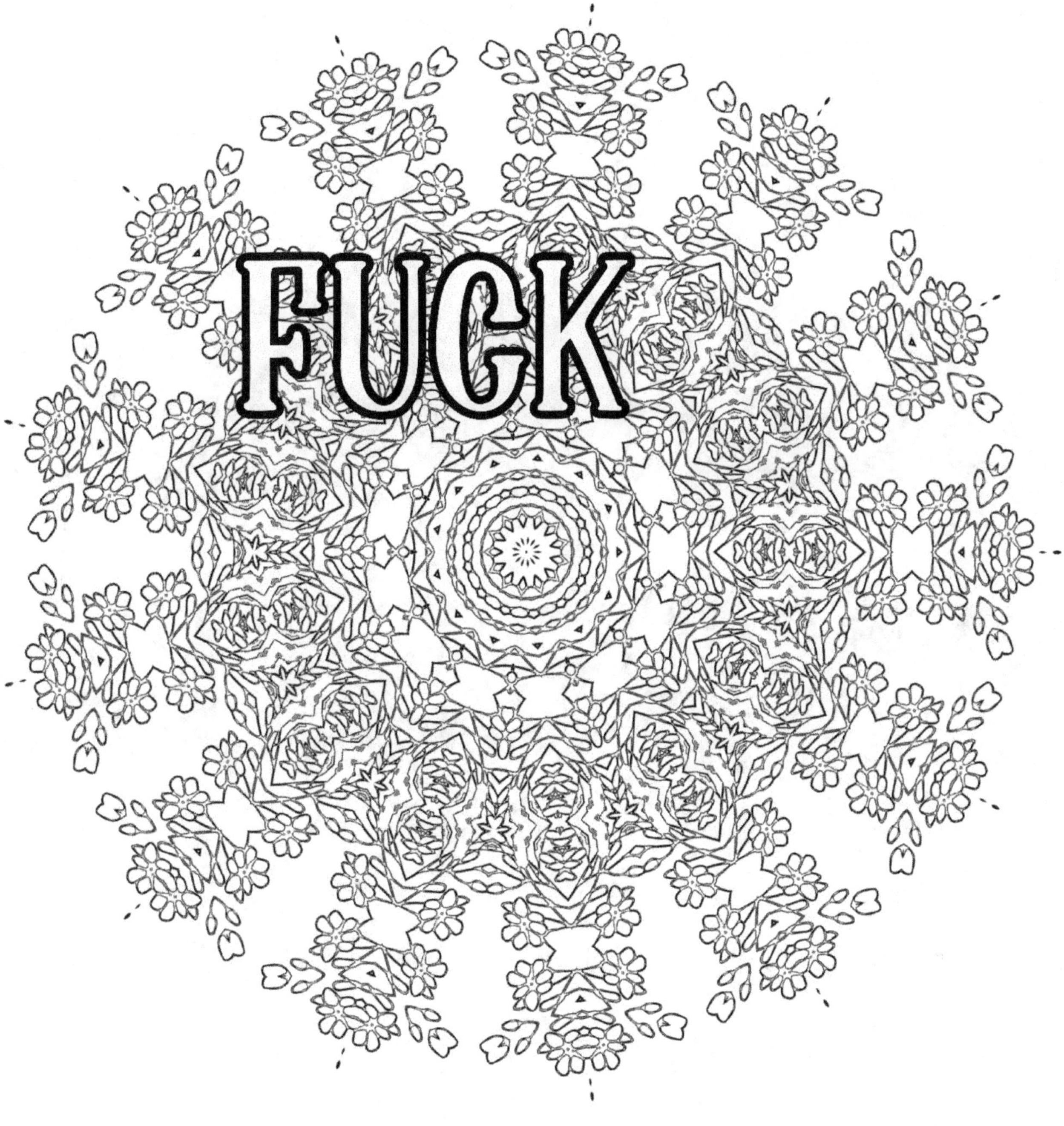
FUCK

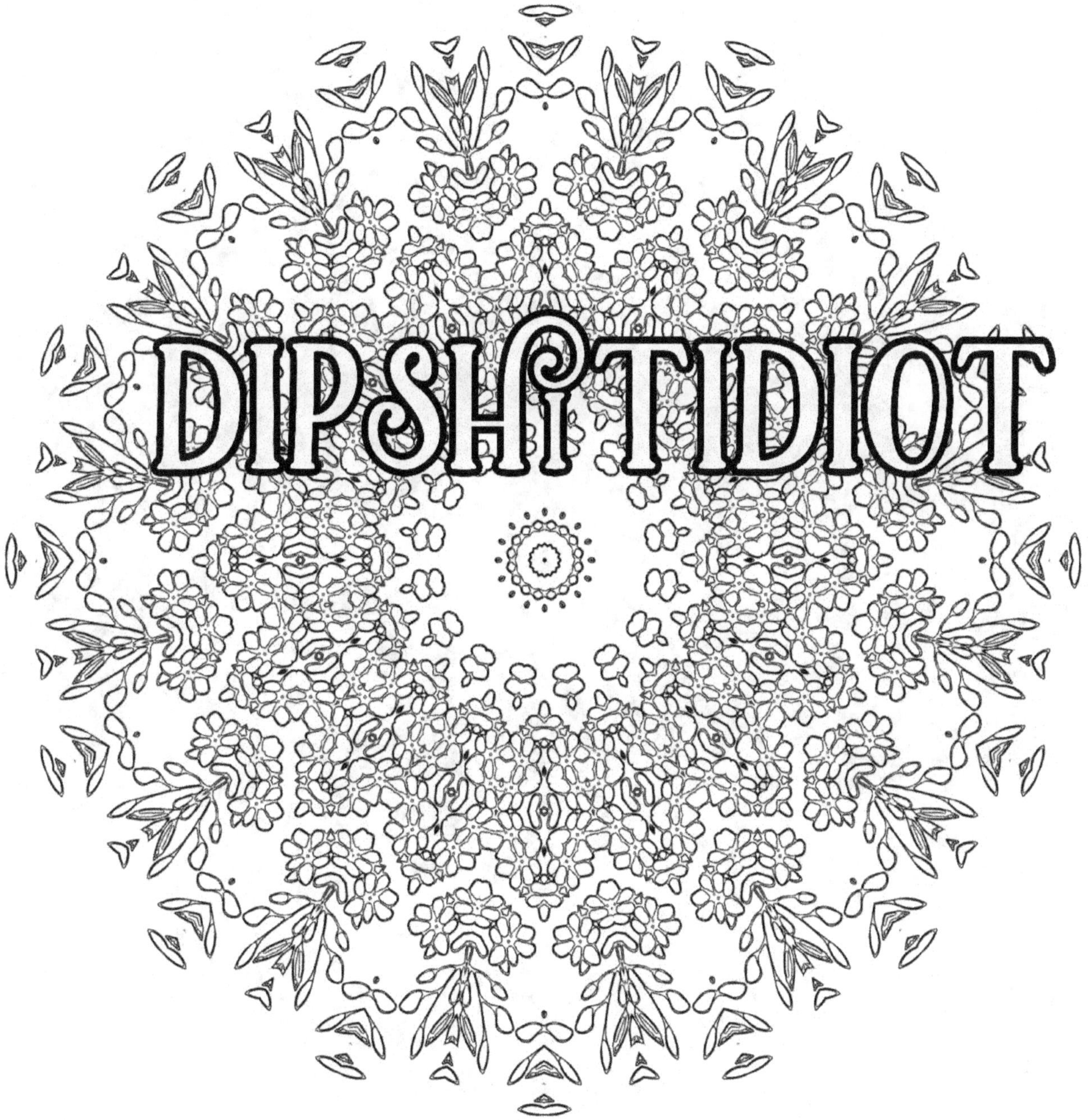
DIPSHIT IDIOT

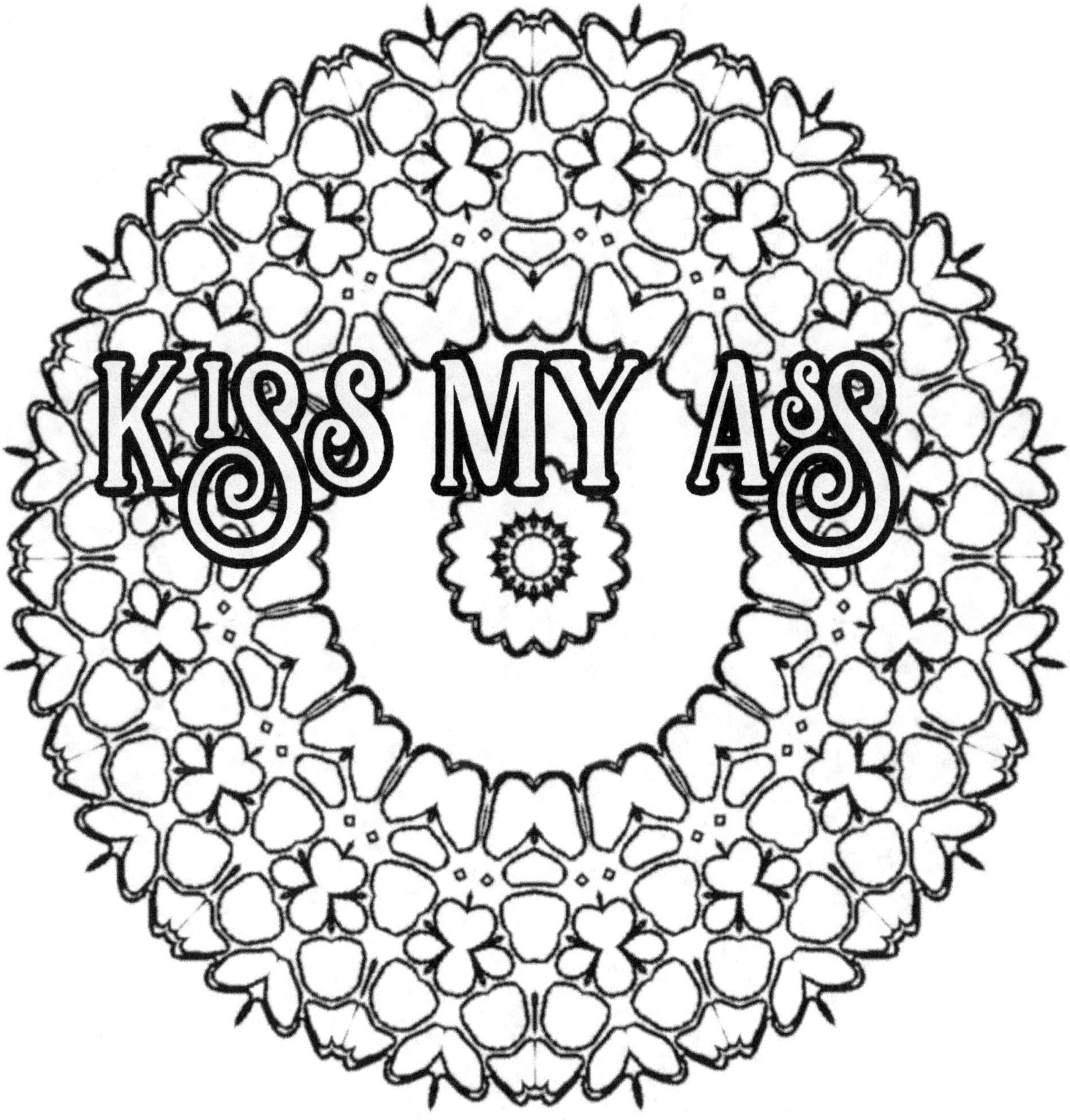
KISS MY ASS

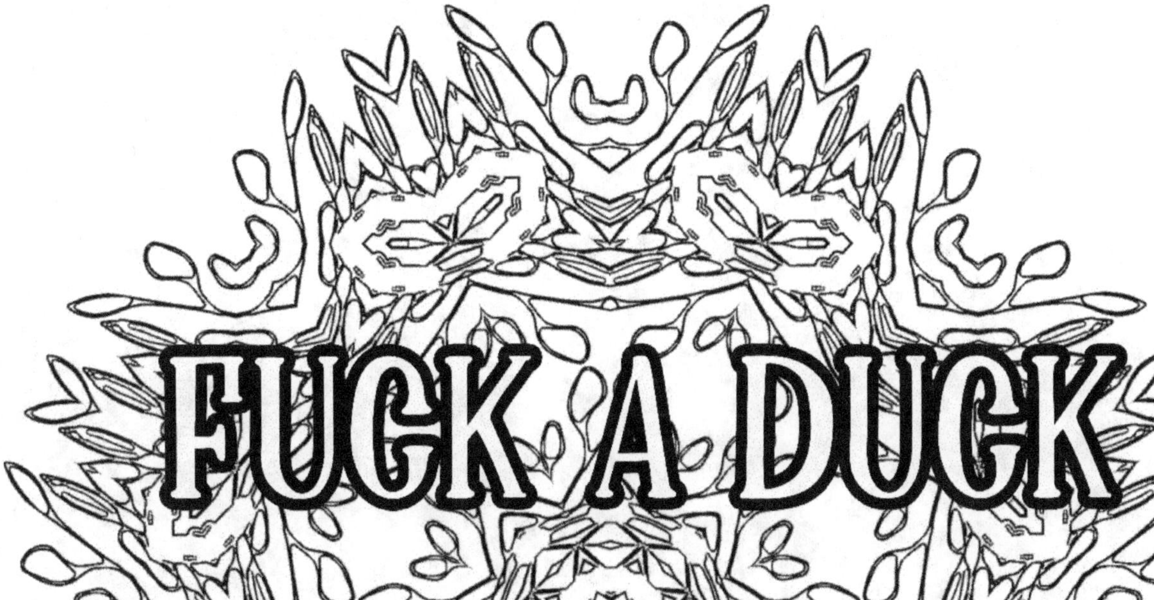
FUCK A DUCK

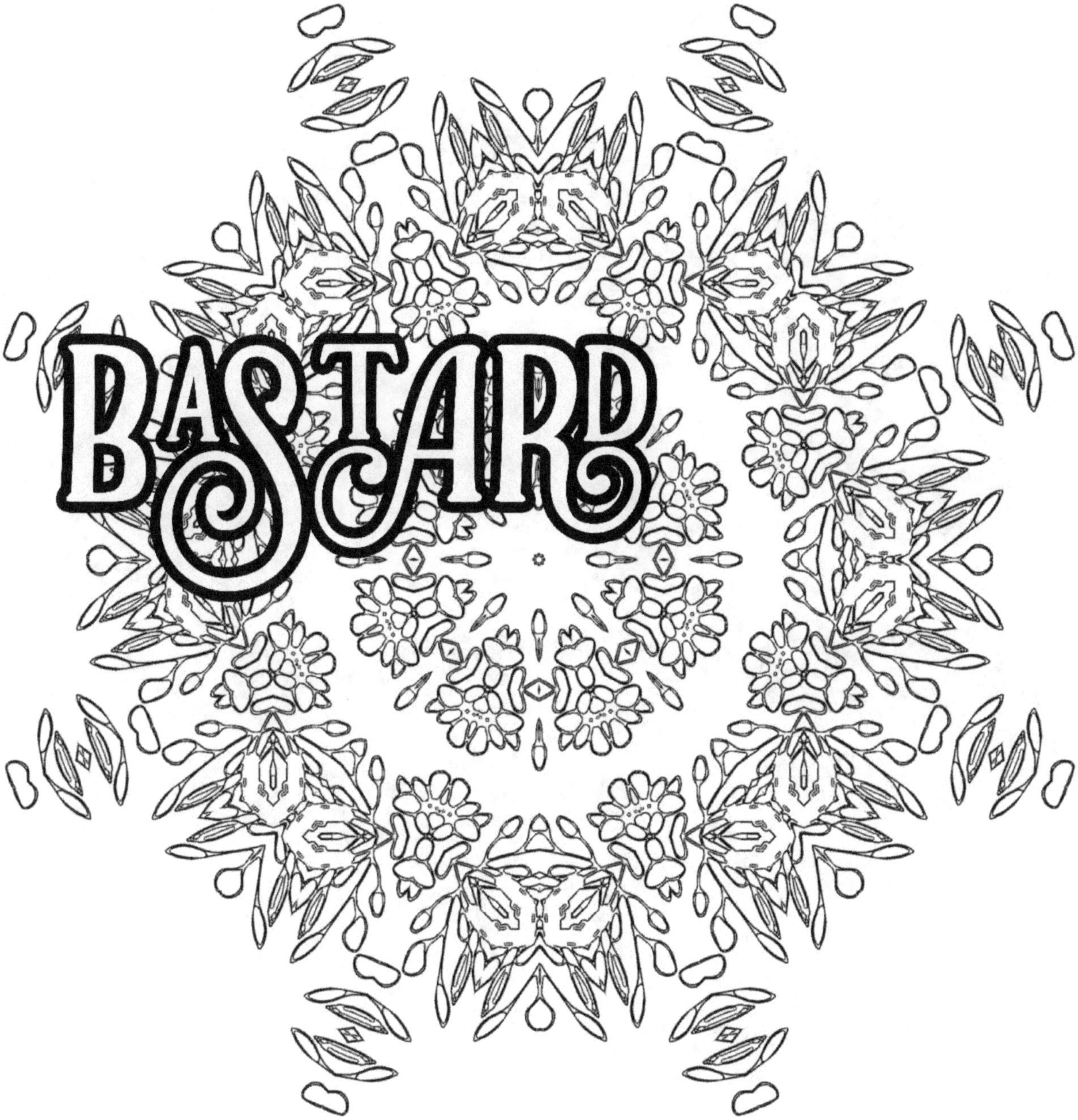
BASTARD

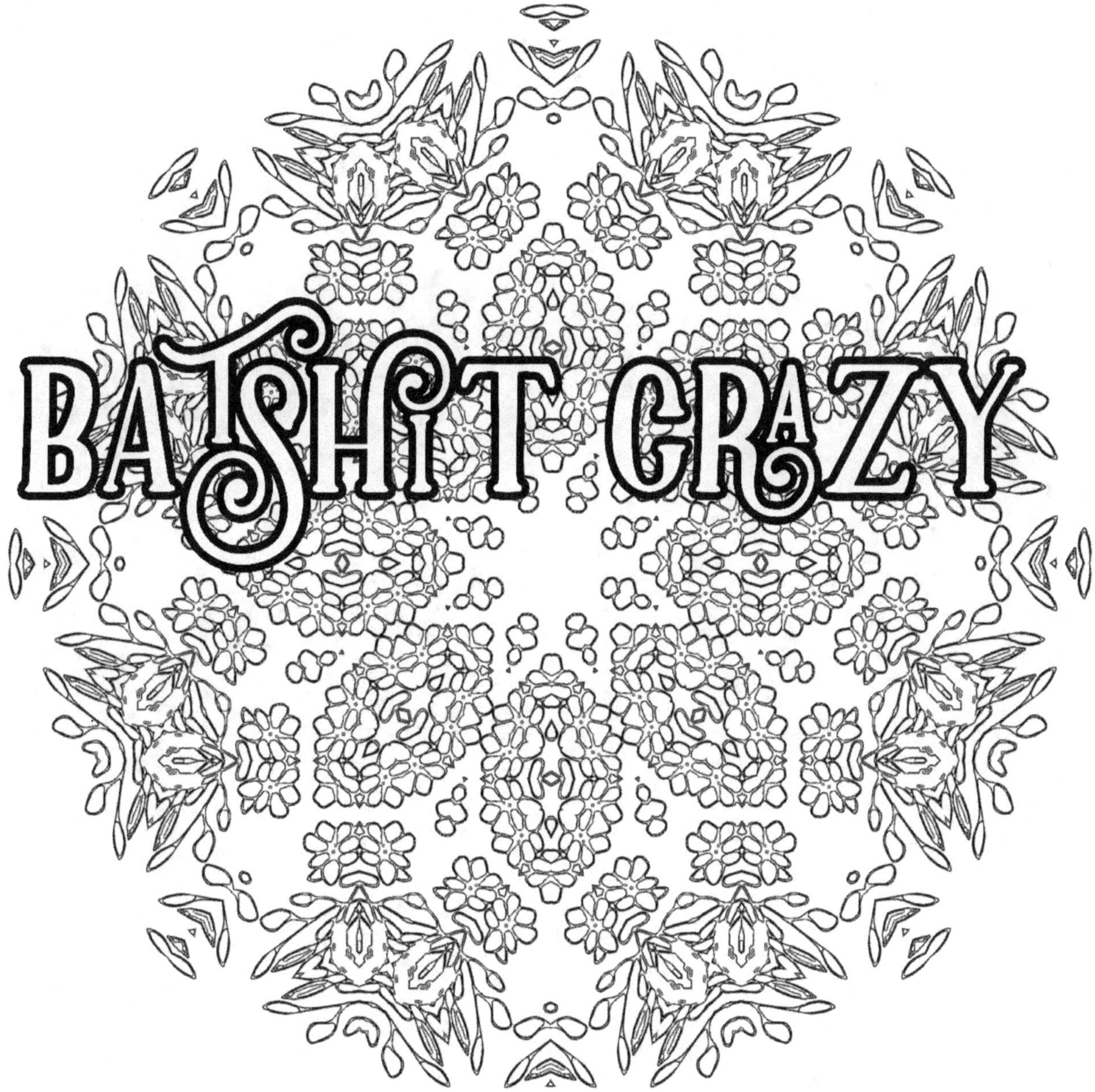
BATSHIT CRAZY

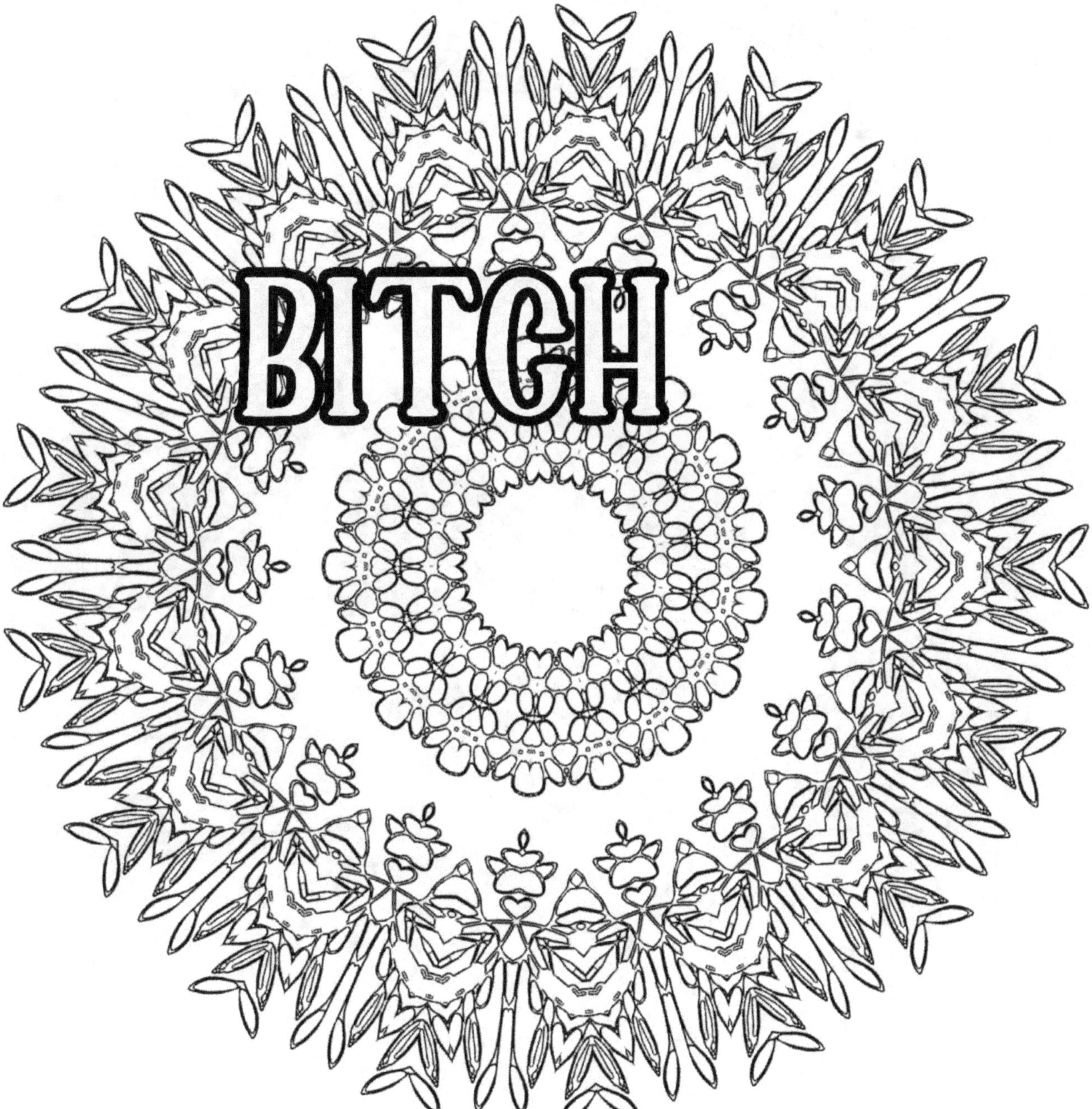
BITCH

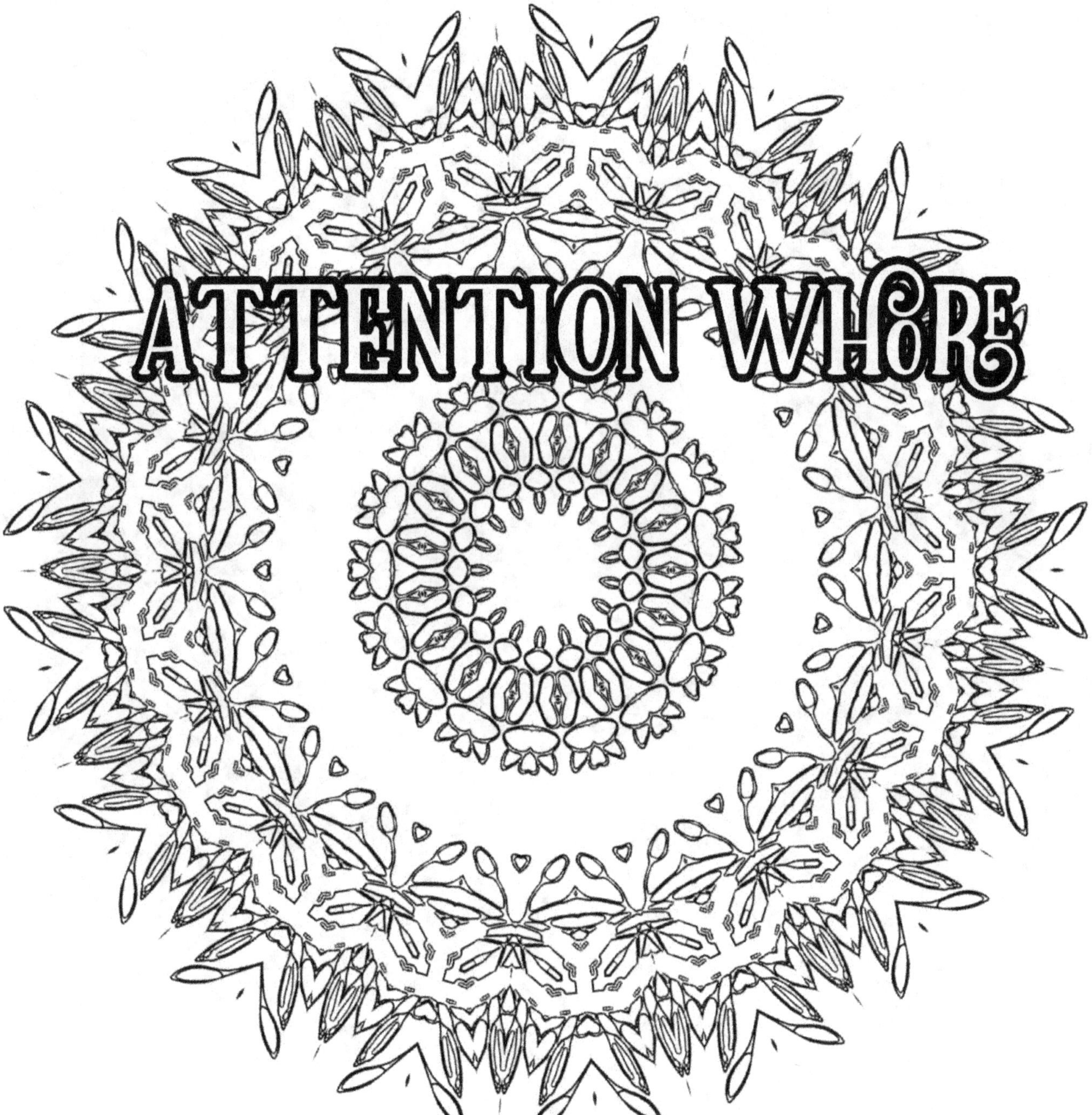
ATTENTION WHORE

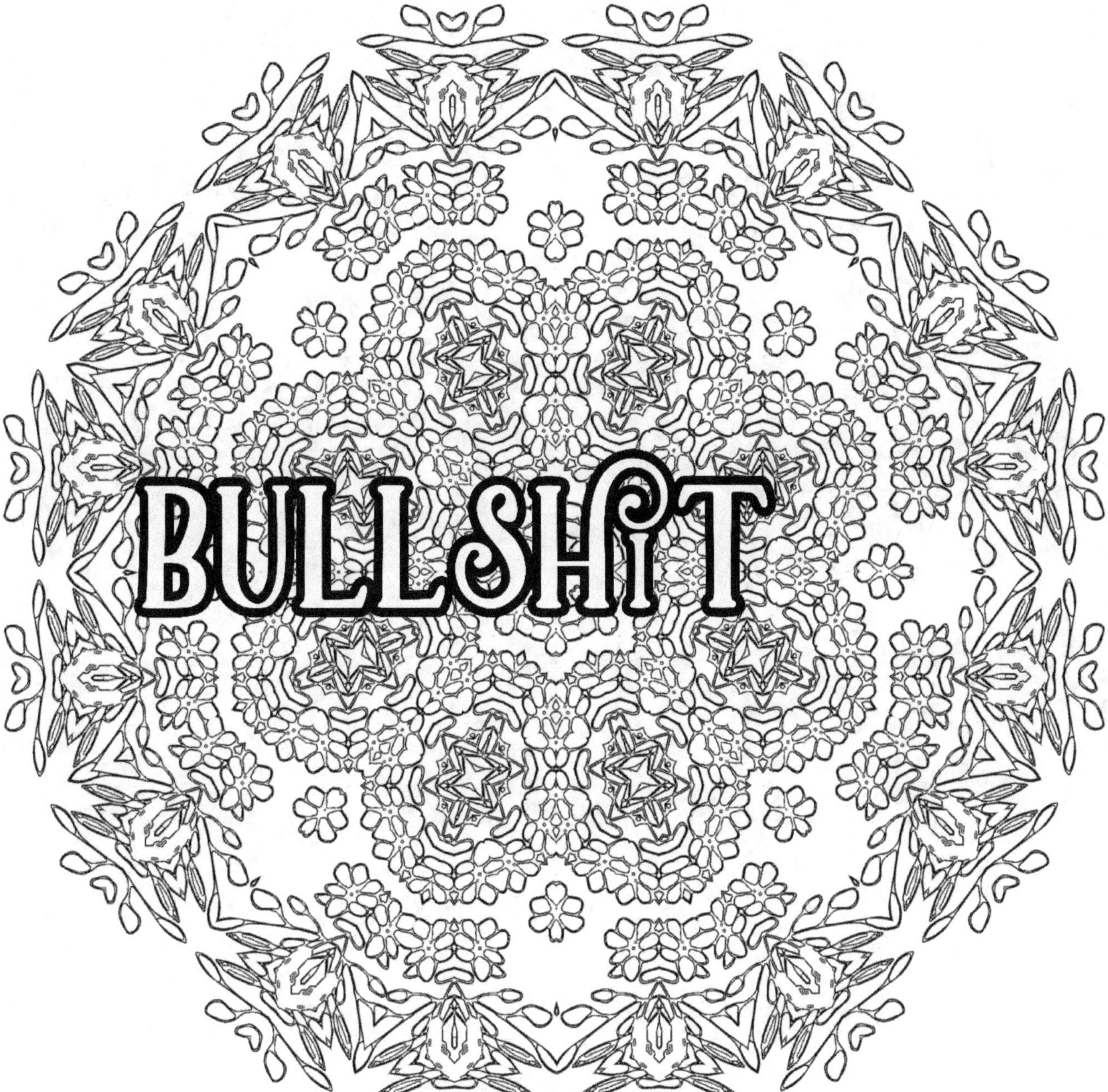
BULLSHIT

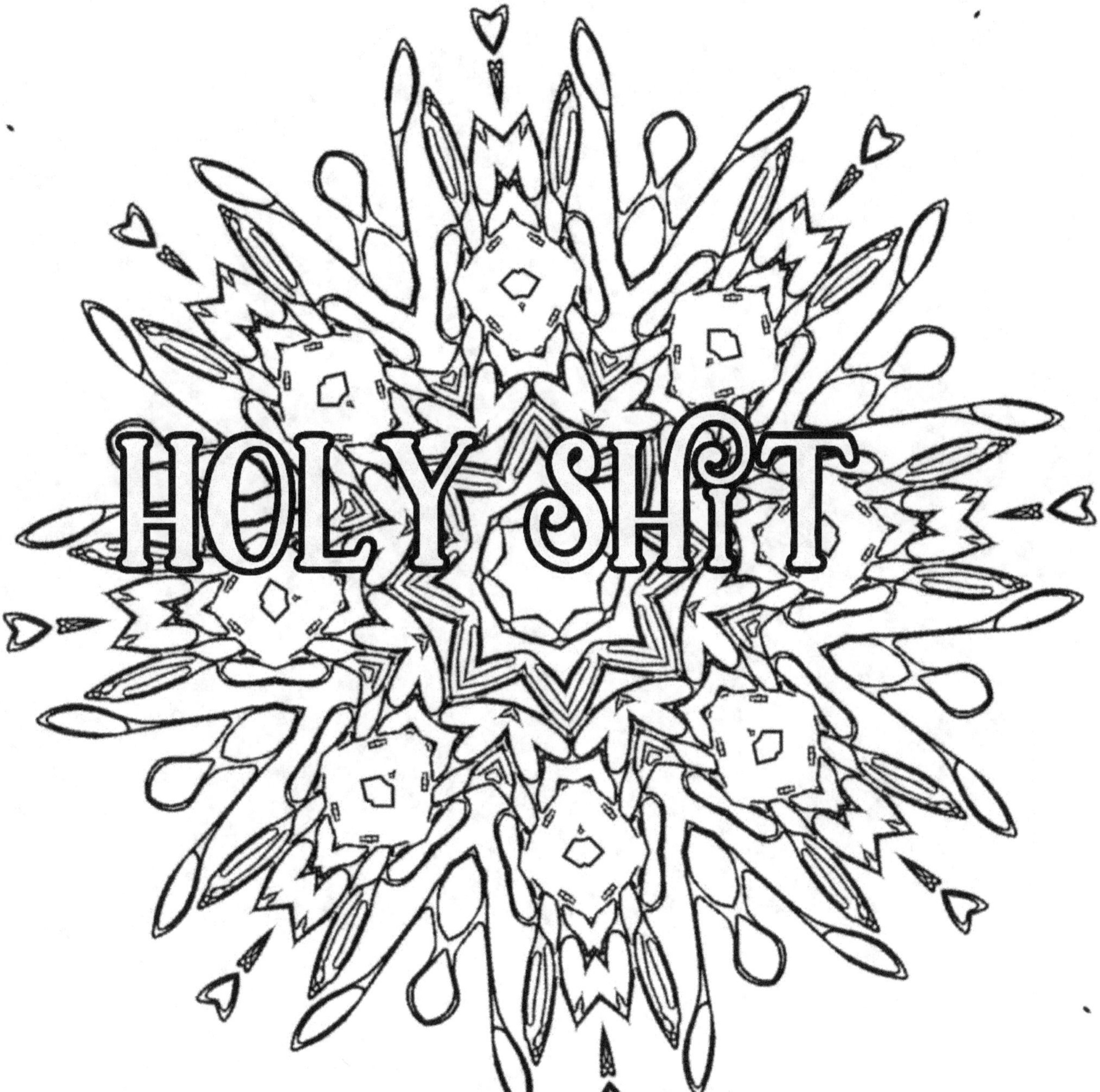
HOLY SHiT

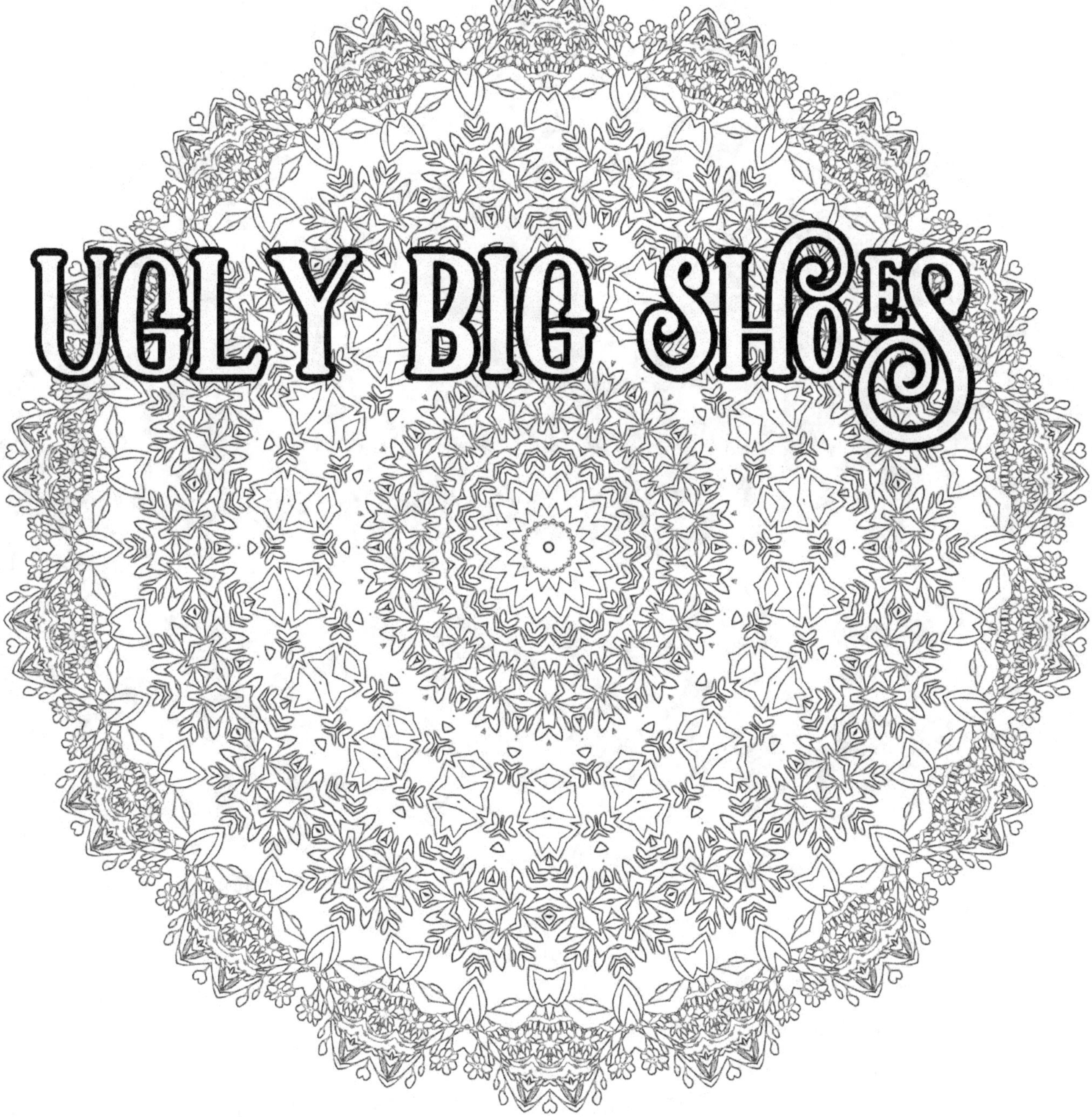
UGLY BIG SHOES

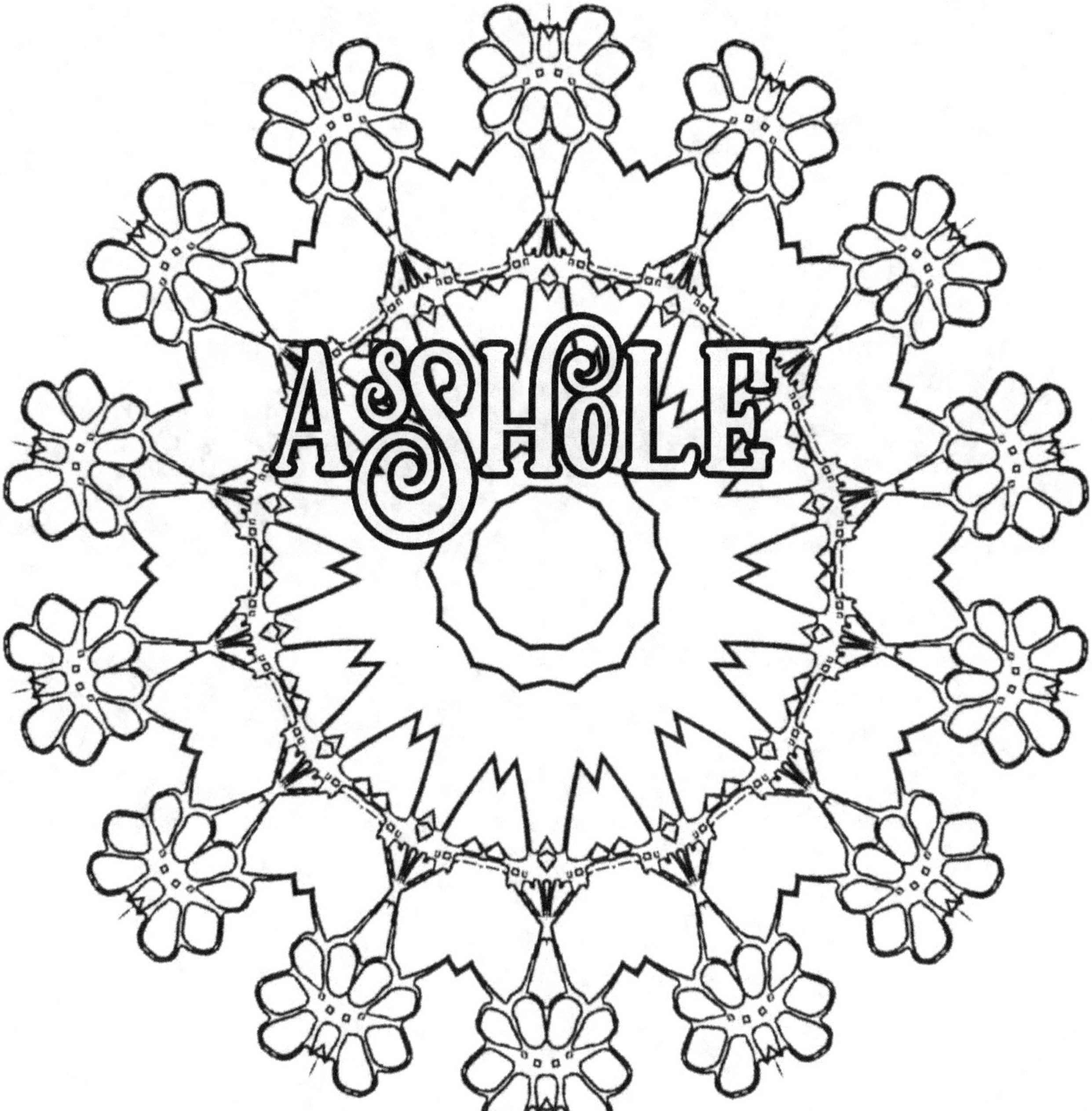
ASSHOLE

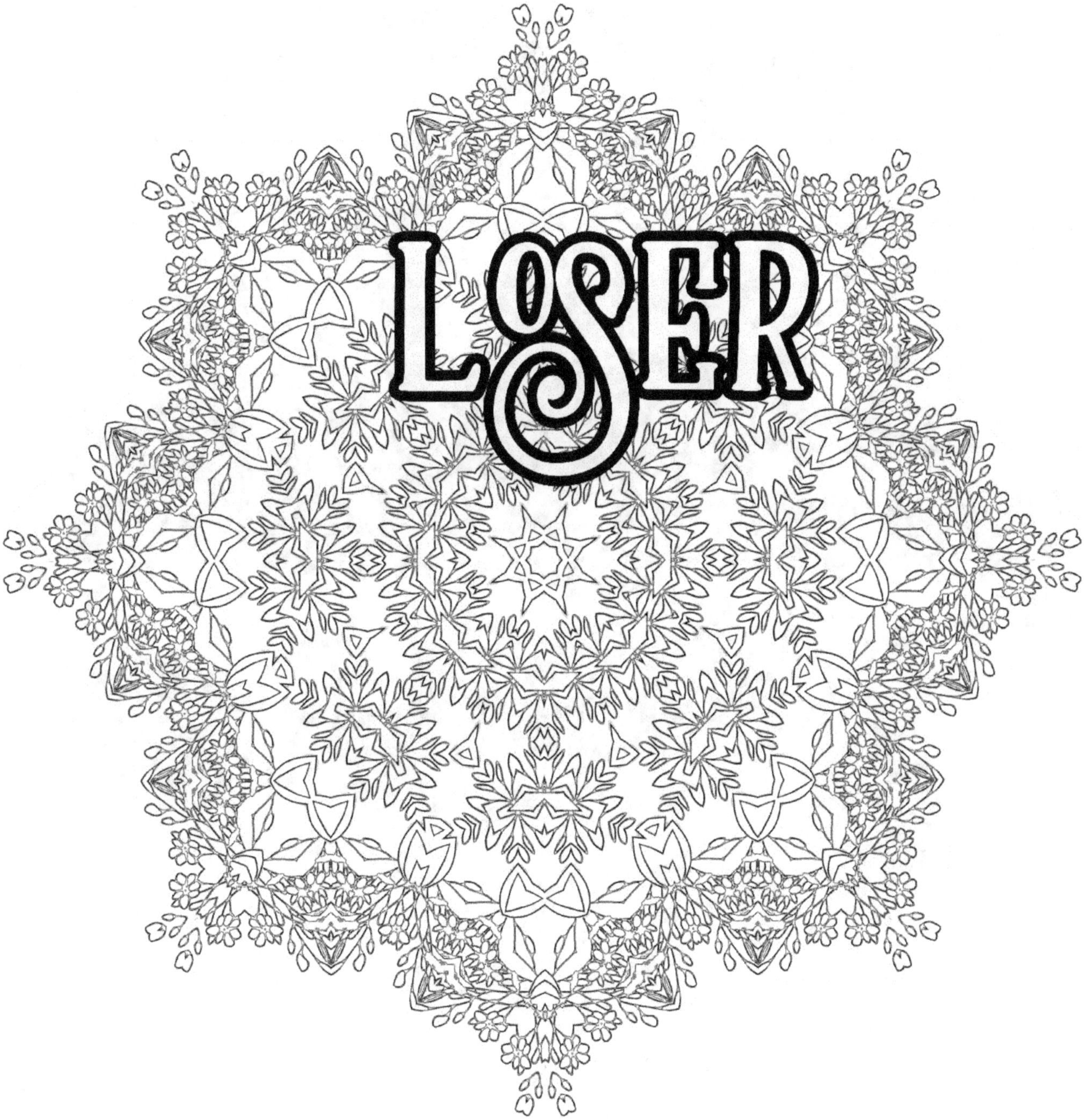
LOSER

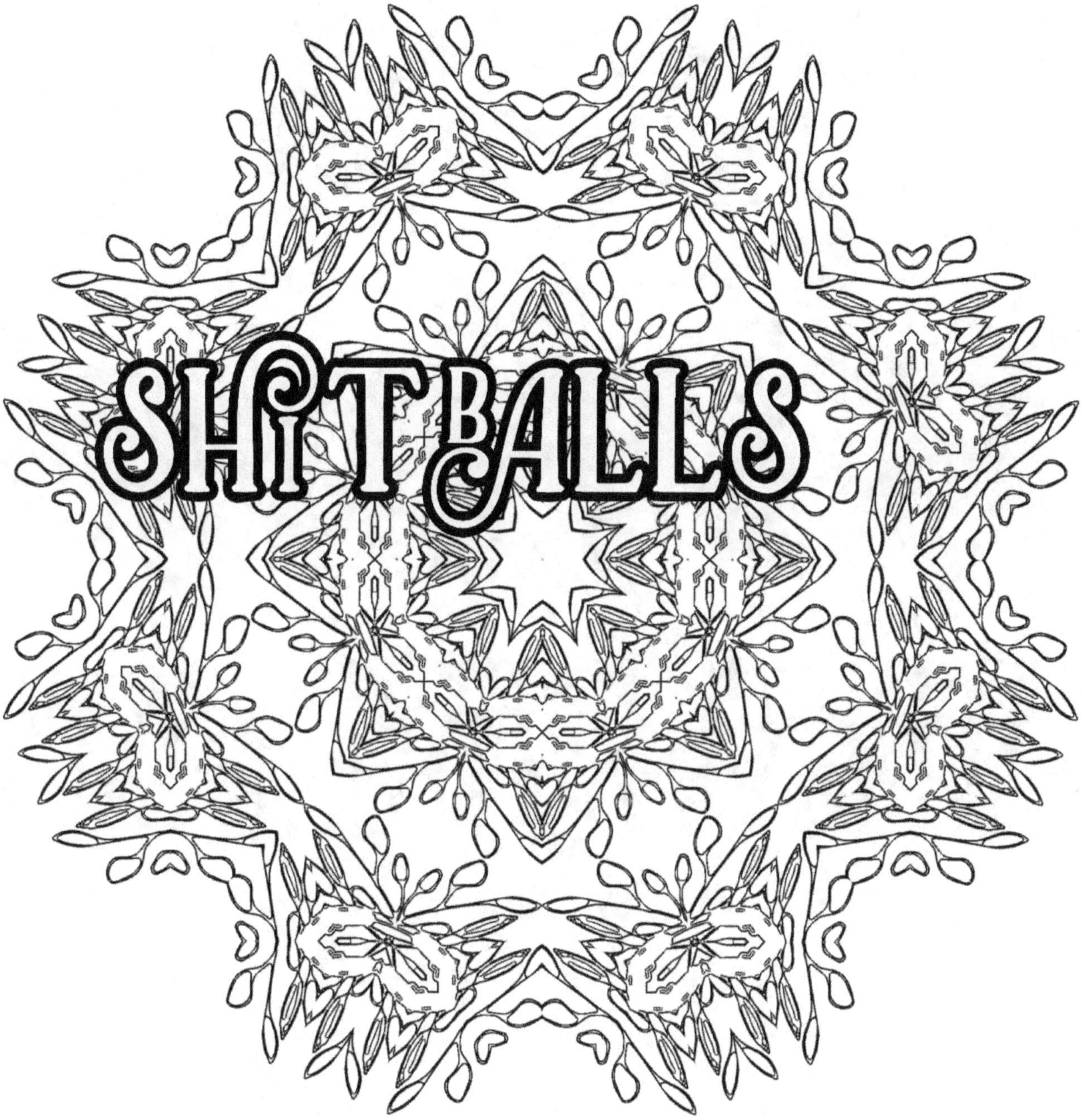
SHIT BALLS

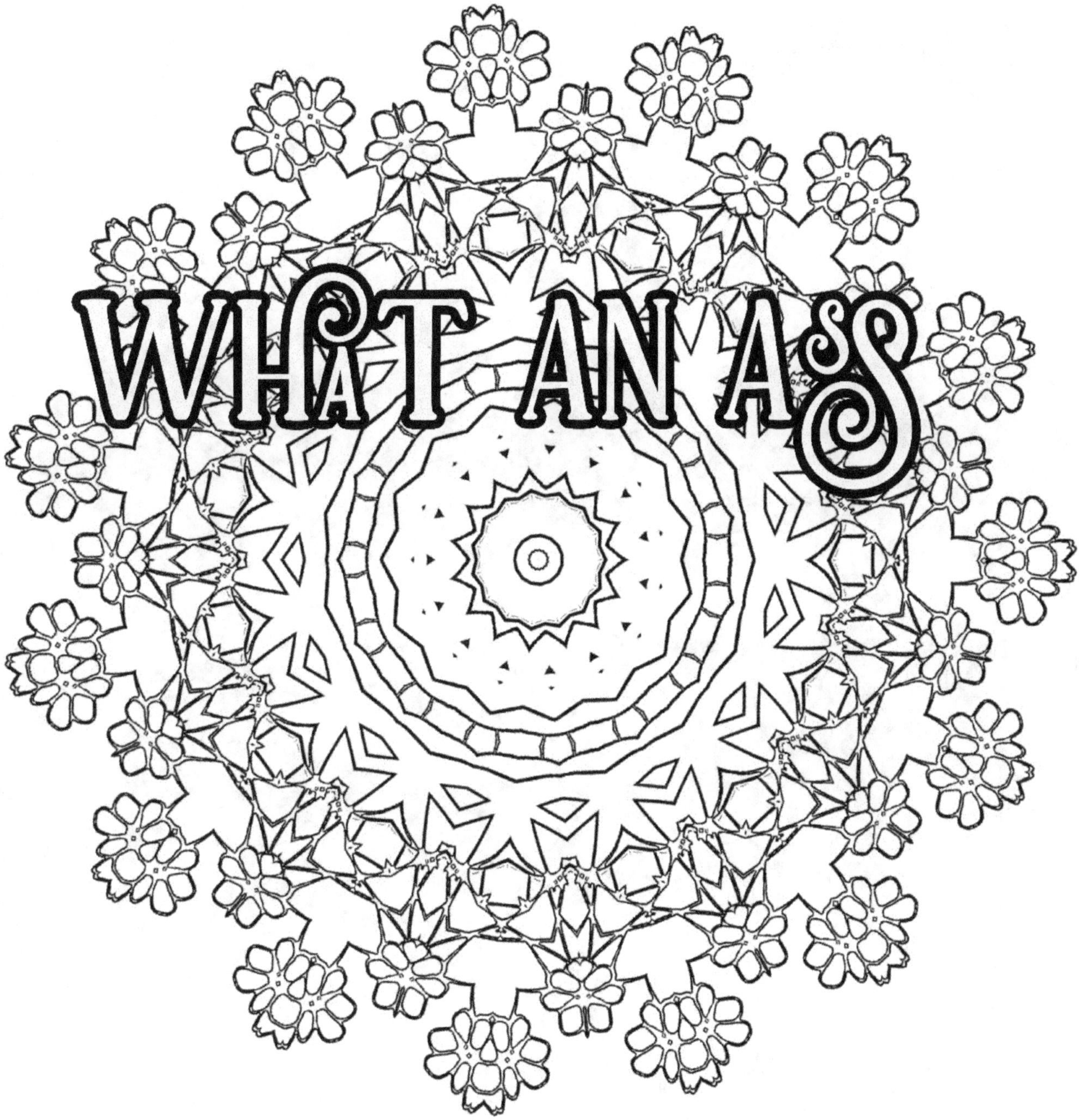
WHAT AN ASS

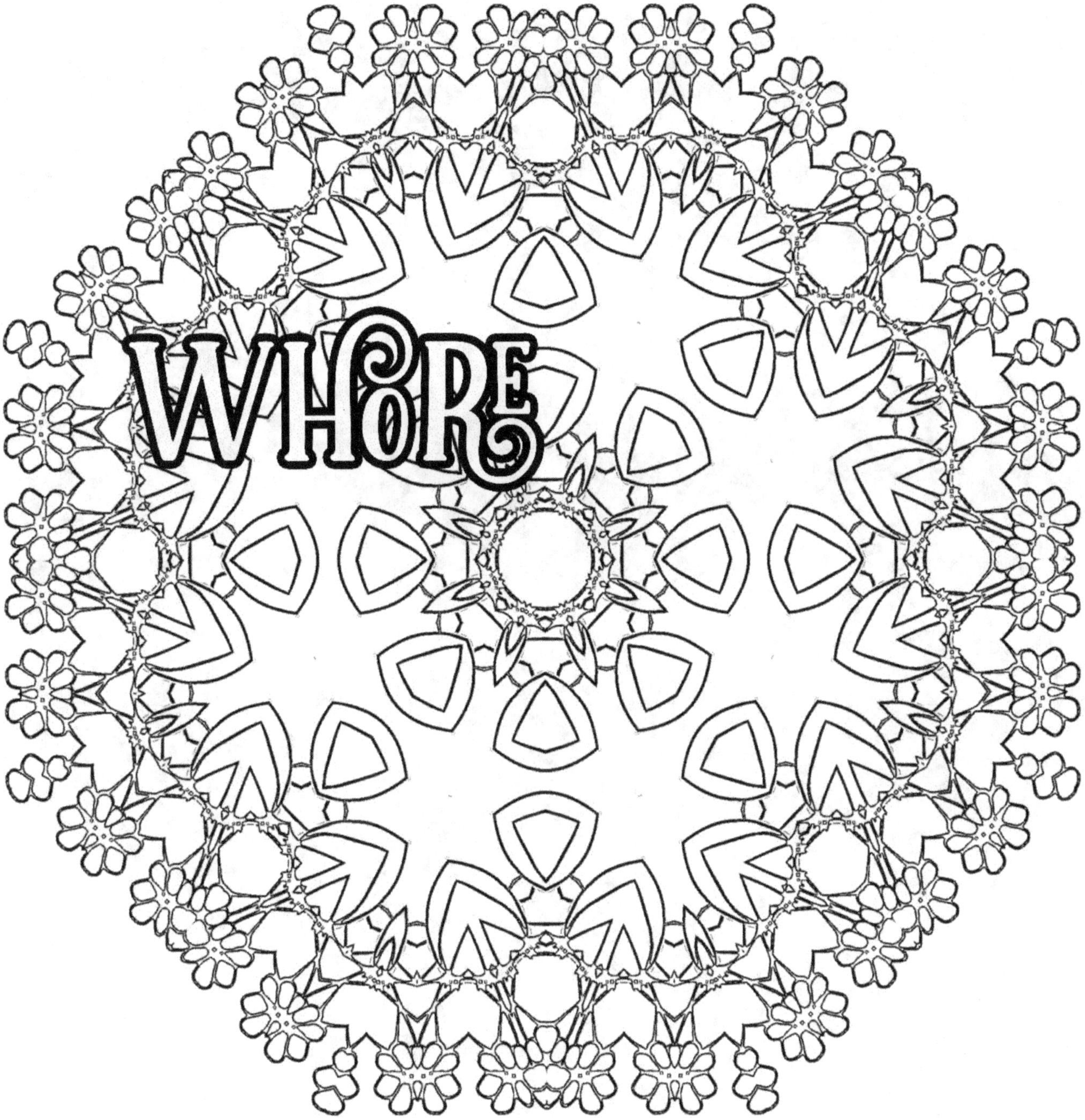
WHORE

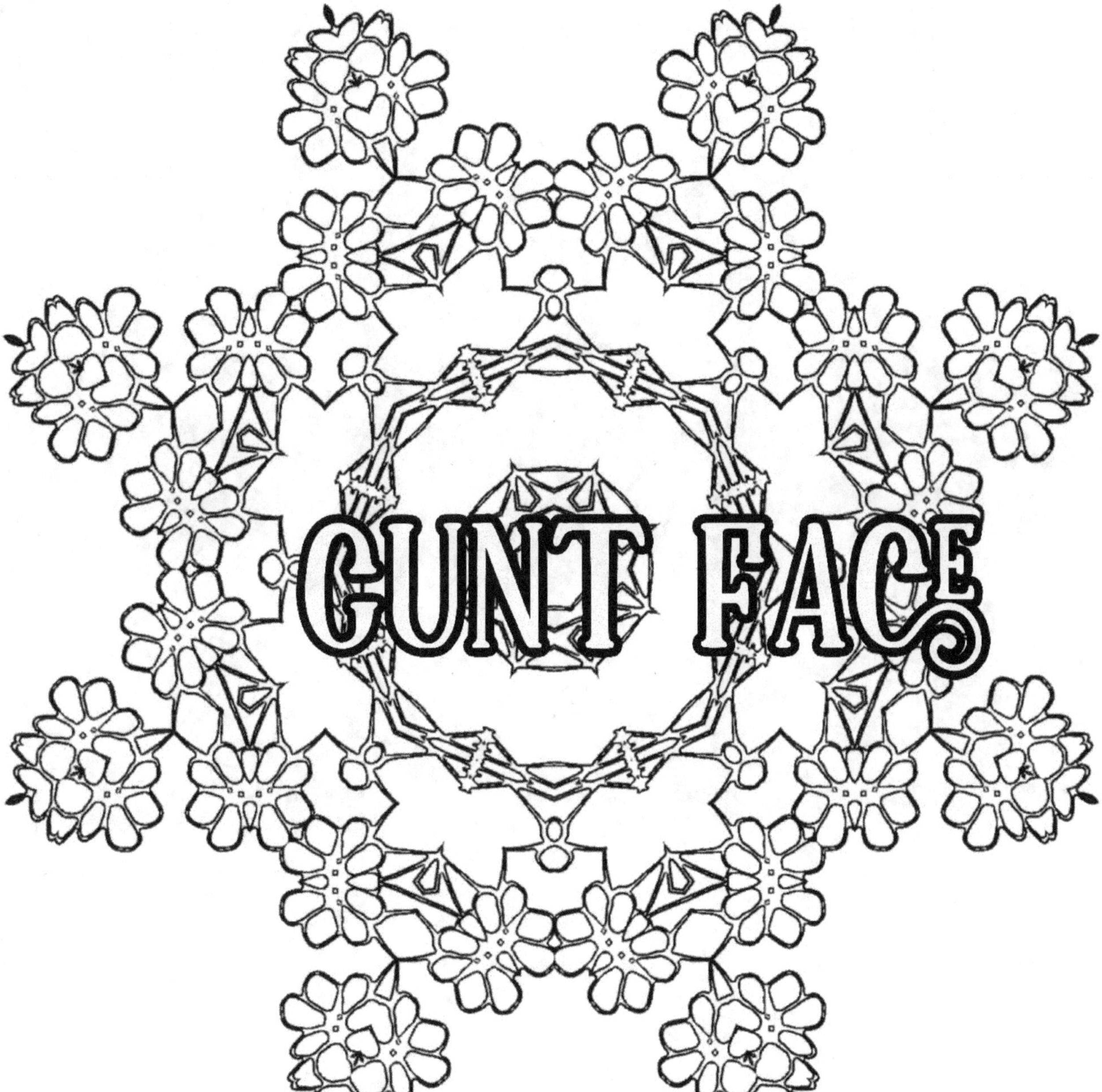
CUNT FACE

www.ingramcontent.com/pod-product-compliance
Lightning Source LLC
Chambersburg PA
CBHW081131180526
45170CB00008B/3065